GONE MAN SQUARED

Poems 1959-1967

by

ROYSTON ELLIS

KICKS BOOKS
NEW YORK, NEW YORK

Published in 2013 by Kicks Books
PO Box 646 Cooper Station
New York NY 10276

Printed in the United States of America

ISBN: 978-0-9659777-9-1

Editor: Miriam Linna
Design: Patrick Broderick/Rotodesign

www.kicksbooks.com

So give the saint his due.
—Love,
John Lennon

His lines are full of uninhibited expressions of the sort of love that so far can only express itself in sex. He has a robust power of expression."

A fierce recording eye.

Exhilarating.

MEMORIES & REMEMBRANCES

BY JIMMY PAGE

I CAN HARDLY BELIEVE the passage of time since I first worked with Royston Ellis more than 50 years ago.

As a young man I was deeply influenced by both the Delta Blues music from America and the written word.

Royston had a particularly powerful impact on me when I first read Gone Man Squared. It was nothing like I had ever read before and it conjured the essence and energy of its time. He had the same spirit and openness that the Beat poets in America had.

When I was offered the chance to back Royston I jumped at the opportunity, particularly when we appeared at the Mermaid Theatre in London in 1961. It was truly remarkable how we were breaking new ground with each reading.

We knew that American Jazz musicians had been backing poets during their readings. Jack Kerouac was using piano to accompany his readings, Lawrence Ferlinghetti teamed with Stan Getz to bring poetry and jazz together.

Playing this type of fusion made me listen very carefully to everything that Royston was saying, it was critical to what I played as I listened with my mind and ears as to what was being read and said, adding a musical interpretation.

It has been a joy for me to sit here and look back at my memories and those wonderful remembrances I have of those early gigs.

Royston, thank you so much for the opportunity then and for the friendship that has followed all these years.

—Jimmy Page

INTRODUCTION

BY

ROYSTON ELLIS

"To write first and think afterwards is still his bad habit," a teacher wrote on my homework when I was nine. "Verbal diarrhoea," was another comment on a school essay when I was 14.

I was cured of my tendency for ceaseless outpouring of words by that teacher's remark. I discovered the beauty of controlled creation; the need to make every word in a poem valuable. A poem is brevity.

By the time I was 18, John Betjeman, the doyen of British mid-20th century poets, in a review of my first selection of poems, *Jiving To Gyp*, commented, "He has a robust power of expression."

I never had doubts about the future: I knew I was going to be a poet. I loved the way words could be scrambled around on paper to produce alliteration, rhythm, rhymes and reason, in solo form: a *poem*.

In the 1950s we used ink fountain pens to write (as I still do) and the use of ballpoint pens was banned at school. For me, composing a poem using a fountain pen was a joyful, adventurous artistic event. One never knew where the hand that held the pen would lead. The flurry and flow of words, and space, across the page was as much part of the poem's structure as its words and message.

Message? When I was 19 and performing my poetry to rock 'n' roll music ("Rocketry"), an intense journalist asked me, "What's your message?"

I hadn't a clue what he meant. My poems were descriptions with a beat, not a beat crusade. But by then I was pigeonholed as a "beat" poet, dubbed by the press as "Britain's beatnik king." I needed a message.

That's the message; there isn't one.

How did a British beat poet begin? Being born in Britain, in Pinner, a leafy dormitory suburb of London in the aptly named county of Middlesex, was my start. It was in 1941 during the Second World War and my first playful years were frequently interrupted by the wail of air raid warning sirens and bombings.

I was the third son of a solicitor's clerk who commuted by train every day to work in chambers in London. My two brothers were both more than 10 years older than me, so I had their influence to encourage my intelligence and the indulgence of my patient mother to tolerate my weirdness. It was certainly considered weird that I should want to scribble words all day.

One poem remains from those days, written in 1956 for my brother who by then, having become a student in Canada, was doing a stint as an artic explorer. It begins:

Alone the white snow glistens
The wind stops still and listens
To the ice, heaving and pitching
And ditching
Into the sea

At 15, and still at school as the sex urge stirred, I was becoming aware that there was an alternative to the bourgeois, suburban, white middle-class complacency into which I was born. I recognised that I was one of the new generation of teenagers emerging in the mid-1950s, a decade after the horrors and deprivation of the Second World War.

The change was apparent in the music we listened to on the radio. Crooners were crooning their way to the sunset while a new beat burst like a bright new dawn. In common with kids then I was enthralled by the beat of the music of Bill Haley and Elvis Presley. The songs were like a light that sparked a rebellion against the old ballroom music – and the old conventions.

The teenage rebellion that drove us was a reaction against parents who were remote, and against those grey, post-war years. Beat music was ours and it fired us with a determination to yield to our desires and express ourselves.

The film *Blackboard Jungle* showed us what we were supposed to do to the new music. Youngsters were seen bopping in their schoolroom to a background of a honking saxophone and a reedy voice exhorting them to: *"One o'clock, two o'clock, three o'clock, rock!"* If school were only like that!

Mine wasn't. I rebelled. I quit. There was a period of reflective darkness in my life and I emerged transformed from being a misfit schoolboy into a farmer's boy milking cows and shovelling shit on a farm in Malpas, Cheshire. That encounter with reality released me from my boring, suburban destiny.

When I realised that inwardly I was free... free... free...! I returned to school, took the compulsory leaving exams and – at last aged 16 – officially left. I celebrated my liberty in a pub, drinking rum-and-black (rum with blackcurrant cordial, the drink of choice for aspiring beat rebels). The next day, wracked with the remorse of my first hangover, I lay in bed and resolved that henceforth I was a poet.

I had nothing to show for my ambition but phrases and rhythmic lines that I had written in my notebooks. Yet I knew that I was at the start of something great, and beat music and poetry were involved. My conventional upbringing – and labouring on the farm – had empowered me with a strong work ethic. (Unusual for the image I was to assume as a bearded, longhaired, scruffy, beat.)

I couldn't be a poet without poems; so I settled down to write. My first published poem written when I was 15 and showing the influence of the farm as well as of protest, appeared in a weekly national newspaper called *Peace News*.

Called *To a freely fighting soldier,* it shows influence of Dylan Thomas too:

The laughing sun wept tears of rain.
The ice-cold blue sky was stabbed with pain,
And the lightning struck the bird-singing trees
As the hat-whisking wind tripped up hives of bees
            And the worm-turd grass spewed up
            the sods
            In the mad crunching fury of tribal gods.

            The tearful sun soon smiled again,
            The thundering sky is earth's cool brain,

And the lightning-struck branches no
one sees
As the hat-whisking wind becomes gentle
breeze,
And the peaceful grass green-warmly nods
In the calm sipping coolness of tribal gods.

As nature changes
Man's destiny ranges,
Perhaps not to return
To the peace that you spurn.

I was agog at the world I found around me.
I started work; first as a technician in a film
studio's sound library where my anxious father
had secured the job for me, hoping my evolving
literary talent could be turned to lucrative
script writing. Of course I left, resorted to my
countryside instincts and became a labourer for
a landscape gardener, and then a bottle washer
in a milk-bottling plant.

Eventually I became a shop assistant in a
famous artist's supply shop in London's Soho,
the centre of what we called then a "bohemian
existence." This, unnoticed by us at the time,
morphed (thanks to the influence of the USA on
the language) into a "beat" lifestyle.

In Soho I frequented clubs featuring
musicians playing what they called traditional
jazz, based on black music from New Orleans.
Rock and skiffle were descendants from this
same source of Blues and became part of my
musical background.

But it was the people enjoying this music that
fascinated me. When I went to parties with kids
of similar taste I would spend much of my time

crouching in a corner jotting down glib phrases describing the action around me, instead of actually taking part in all the drinking, jiving and snogging.

The music, and the crowd who followed it, and the sexual encounters encouraged by our "free love" spirit, yielded rich material for a budding beat poet. Gradually these poems about the bohemian Beat scene and about the musical Big Beat scene, became my introduction to the dawn of London's "swinging sixties."

In 1959 my poem, *Gone Man Squared* appeared in *Beat* magazine. It did not occur to me then that I had become part of the Beat Generation, because I didn't know it existed. Although I frequently took to the road and hitchhiked throughout the country on a whim, as did the beats of the USA, I had not read Kerouac or Ginsberg.

It was only later, in May 1973 in a letter published in the *International Times*, that John Lennon claimed that I had been influenced by Ginsberg.

Now we all know, Miles, that Allen is an important figure in our 'culture,' but you/he don't need to 'backdate' his influence. By the way, the first dope, from a Benzedrine nose inhaler, was given to the Beatles (John, George, Paul & Stuart) by an (in retrospect) obviously "English cover version" of Allen – one Royston Ellis, known as 'beat-poet' (he read poetry whilst we played 12-bar blues at the local in-place!).

So give the saint his due.
Love, John Lennon

My 'beat' in 1959 when the first of the poems in this book were published in *Jiving To Gyp* (*gyp* means hell) was beat music. But because I had a beard and led a bohemian lifestyle (of no fixed abode) and wrote poetry, I was tagged a 'beat' – beatnik was the term then – without realising that's what I had become.

Although I didn't comprehend it at the time, it was more than coincidence that the publisher of my poetry in England – Scorpion Press – was the UK distributor of Ferlinghetti's City Lights Books, the publishers of *Howl* by Allen Ginsberg and of other US beat poets.

I moved into a beat commune in Chepstow Villas, Nottinghill Gate, London, that was presided over by the writer Cressida Lindsay (1930-2010) whose boyfriend was a rent boy called Mark Hyatt (1940-1973). He was a genuine embryo beat poet as he was barely literate but loved the words he could formulate on an old typewriter and typed and spaced them according to his moods.

We survived by "totting" – patrolling the streets of West London with a pushcart and collecting junk, which we later sold on Saturday mornings at a stall in London's famous Portobello Road street market.

There was a nearby pub where older poets like my mentor at the time, Sir John Waller (1917-1995) and John Gawsworth (1912-1970), the King of Redonda, a title he inherited from fantasy writer M.P.Shiel (1865-1947), would gather and regale us about literary bohemia.

I wanted young people to read – or at least hear – my poems. But that seemed impossible as young people hardly cared about reading newspapers, let alone poetry. I decided I needed to promote my poetry properly, like a pop star. Thus I joined up with The Drifters who later became The Shadows and backed the teenage pop idol of the time, Cliff Richard. We appeared at a few teenage raves and on television.

I was eventually pitched into national consciousness by remarks I made in a television programme about youth called *Living for Kicks*, shown nationwide in Britain in March 1960. Suddenly I was notorious: the beatnik with a beard no mother would want her daughter to go out with.

Surfing the momentum this wave of fame gave me, I took to the road for performances of rocketry. I conspired with musicians I met on the way to back me. One was a teenage guitarist called Jimmy Page and we did several television and stage shows (including a notable one at London's Mermaid Theatre) with Jimmy playing his own compositions for my poems.

When I visited Liverpool in June 1960 to perform at the invitation of the Guild of Undergraduates at Liverpool University, I encountered and appeared with a group of four teenagers (John, Paul, George and Stuart). I wanted them to come to London to accompany me and, when John Lennon told me his name for the group was Beetles (because he liked the Beetle Volkswagen car), I said that because they liked the beat way of life, played beat music and I was a beat poet, why not spell the name with an "A."

They didn't come to London and went instead to Hamburg. John asked me to go with him as a sort of poetical compere for the group but I declined. I did leave England, though. I hitched a lift to Moscow where I appeared on stage with Russia's most popular young poet at the time, Yevgeni Yevtushenko, and in 1961 bummed around Berlin as the Berlin wall was being built.

My travels gave me a thirst for new places as I realised there was another world, free for me as a poet to taste. I stayed for a while in the Channel Islands before moving, in 1963, to Las Palmas in the Canary Islands for three years.

It was there that the last of these poems (*The Cherry Boy*) were written, a commentary on the beat life of my youth.

I continued to travel, spending 16 years on Dominica in the Caribbean before settling in 1980 in Sri Lanka. Here I live the life of an erstwhile beat poet, in a 110 year-old cottage in an orchard of papaya, coconuts and bananas, overlooking the Indian Ocean. I have become indeed "a gone man squared."

Royston Ellis
Sri Lanka 2013
www.roystonellis.com

CONTENTS

JIVING TO GYP
1959

For Cliff—a drifter's boy, some rhythm & blues.

First published by the
Scorpion Press in 1959

*This is the sad story of Stephen
and the life he leads, jiving to gyp.*

DID YOU KNOW?

Did you know
that when she died and
swore the only damns she could,
that all the birds
up in the trees
settled down to sleep?

Did you know
that when she screamed and
threw the loaded gun at him,
that all the love
still in his heart
quickly changed to hate?

Did you know that when she posed and
said those kill-me words out loud,
that all the deeds
of any life
vanished with the shot?

JIVING TO GYP

Bloody great this life we lead,
Duckie, you should try it:
Just forget what others say
And find a carefree clique;
Hold callous sexy orgies.
Knock all the willing girls
(But watch Virginia, it's her bad week),
And jive with us to gyp.

• • •

Stephen and sweet describe this lad
sullenly with a clique;
his eyes of reproach and innocence
blink at the jokes of his mates
as he shies from the crude exploitation of
sex
and considers the quivering clock on the
wall
and reckons that time can go to Hell.

Attractive and cursed with beauty
silently all his life;
his mind filled with parental respect
accepts the plans of his mates:
so he flees from the restrictions of disci-
pline
to a fantasy of lethargic behaviour
where people don't bother to bother.

JAZZ CLUB

They go:

Past the patient priestess writing
on her list of intellectuals
who have come to languish and
relinquish all frustrations

Into a Chinese-lanterned room
of casual conversation lost
without reluctance and forgotten
without retaliation

Into a snuggy, smuggy room
of smarting, cancered incense
and callous sly depression
hovering uncertainly,

Into an exclusive frigid room
of bohemian pseudo sultriness –
cute little cliques of callowness
eyeing desperation

Where wistful wilting characters
reacting to the Southern Stompers
friction-frenzied with exhilaration
spurtle-dance and gently jive:
slurred shadows undisturbed by
moodily repentant ginger
singer
anquished and expressioned singing
under the party babble
at the back socks
with the banjo:

Reclining beat hazily
ignored;
tapped to by the bored
and valiantly unconcerned
loose lovers
plotting
amidst the admiration of a car
load of
mumblers baffled by intruders;
St Christopher's disciples
worshipping in lassitude:

Baselsss band with the sousa
phone for fourpence,
hearing jammed,
and all senses
lost with sexes;
creatures agonised with pleasure;
weirdest based on ostentation:

Hair brushed round and round
and randy
never to be parted
from boredom-born delights
with century-entry rounded collars
and haggard looks from party nights,
where Fred bare and still
waters from the windowsill
and climbs into her chest
of drawers:

And so with all the bearded bo's –
extroverts in museum clothes –
and the long-haired penguin-women
walking with an aimless rhythm,
grunts and glows lead to a pub

where bourgeois-bait substantiates
comments on the modern youth
shrugging down a rum-and-black
and
floundering with resentment.

STEPHEN

..."I mean to say I think perhaps
you'll understand me well
when I say that this is what
I had in mind. Oh Hell!"

Dour and sourly chuckle kid
stammer smirk a stout –
lithesome lassitude inclining
blend the trends devout,

Mystic lazy loose and lost
whimper smoke a swish –
church and bastard longingly
eschew a glance a-miss,

Sugar-wise and dandruff whine
mention smack a mate –
disdain and loving greaterness
wear beery bait,

Tease and take the shyly won
wooing sweet a whim –
unattached and influential
incite upright to sin,

Darkly deep a savage virgin
prudent snide a price –
catch the casual prettiness,
winks a-while suffice,
Poke pleasure pure and damn
suffer so a soul -
oily old and artisan
in wretched rigmarole.

... "Which is, could be, I'm pretty sure,
   least that's what I've heard tell
   so perhaps you'll know just what
   I had in mind. Oh Hell!"

• • •

Another (Stephen please
   said Paddy) rum,
I'll be married in three days –
Cheers, old mate –
   I dig you Steve,
   thinks Paddy.

Nice crowded (Excuse me
   laddie) pub
with this pop music playing –
Be fine to jive –
   Then let's do that,
      said Paddy.

Under and (Here! Look at
   these two boys) round –
Watch svelte Stephen's little bum,
It's bloody cute –
   I like this Steve.
      O.K. boys.

You've earned this (Take it or
   I'll do you) drink
a hardman says to Paddy,
then turning round
   to Stephen says:
      for Lulu.

• • •

A withering there
    and a scurrying here
    and a sigh of lovers clinging –

A tittering now
    and a desperate vow
    and a flow of desire intense –

A smothering sweet
    and a terrific heat:
    this is a bastard beginning.

GONE MAN SQUARED

Crawling round the darkness
   of the
Seething vital dungeon,
Pushing past the prisoners
   of the
Listless tapping senses,
Clinging to the weapons
   of the
Coffee wake-me languish:
   Stabbed by the clarinet call,
   Beaten by the drums;
   Skiffled by the washboard
   And sent by the bass;
   Cringing at the crooner,
   Vying with the trumpet,
   Glaring at his partner,
   He jives with the rest.

Making for the exit
   of the
Sweating mothered cellar,
Breaking off the fan-ship
   of the
Writhing nights of going,
Hating all the throbbing
of the
Skipping blues of sadness:
   Defeated by cats' jazzitude,
Rocked by his soul,
Perplexed by his query
And hurt by his hops;
Losing all his coolness,
Fleeing from his haven,

Seeking out the answer,
He rolls to the end.

• • •

Café and coffee use
   up the day:
sitting with Jenny from
   breakfast to pubtime.

They've nothing else to do
   but listen to
      the music
stuttered from the braying juke box
as it Presleys just for kicks;

and gradually swallow
   the pull-in pull-though swill.

They talk to each other
   with grunts and yawns
and flick fags in cups full of sugar

There's nothing to say
   and nothing to do:
   there's nothing.

PARTY

Bearded brothel-bard
       patrols
his sleepy home,

(Absence-temped friends
       arrived
with loving girls),
faithful steady gone
       away
from his desire.

Snogging couples lie
       between
his loneliness:

So bravely he pretends:
he doesn't care a damn.

• • •

And Stephen

slurring and snarling
   and wistfully pretty,
mumbles and stumbles
   as he jives to gyp.

• • •

Grollops blood and wine pure crap
   blending bending breeding bright:
   morning never dreading night
   tending sending daily vigour
   coming with a weekend wanton
   disturbing neighbours damning them.

• • •

Steve cuddled her puppy fat carcass close
to him
and flabbily fumbled
as he thought about nothing
and wanted to spew.

• • •

Pensive and pregnant
because of her sin,
pensive and pregnant
because of him.

• • •

Cuddly sweater
    and trousers typically tapered
tends to cavort in slow rhythmic motion
with a suave and supercilious languor;

Blustery beads
    and piety pulsating in black
hint at a pleasure writhing morosely
with a lustre succinct, salacious and sour:

Drearily gen
    and chuffed with a chuckle by Jenny
helps to suggest an apathy bleeding
with anguish and Satan...
        their jive's rather j.

• • •

Crouching in a taxi
           seven
travelling to spend
           a night
in London
           jiving in a club
in Soho.

Sweating in a fervour
           Stephen
desperate for drink
           smiling
at a man
           pressing to his lips
full bottles.

Scrounging in a fashion
           even
squandering all through
this night
in London
           jiving in a club
in Soho.

SOHO GAME

Two likely lads lean
and lovely
  against a bar
no holes
  and danger-trying
(very)
  while shrugging down vodkas
for bait
  with smarmy barmy music men
who crave
  to escape from that place
for another
  drink all they dare
to seduce
  then bid them goodnight.

ANOTHER PARTY

All the shuts were shop and so
we had to go without
        at Stephen's Christmas party.

I thought you said that you'd got peaches.
No! Pig's kidneys, and the cat's had those.

I feel like ten men, Stevie said,
Nine men dead and one man dying.

The beer's all gone. Then we'll go get some
And if we die we'll meat James Dean in
heaven.

The bed's collapsed under Graham and
Bertha!
How dis-bloody-scusting, Virginia said
as she sank on the sofa with Cecil.

Now here's Jamie with his merrydown Jill
and a ready reaction to riotous talk:
have a crisp, and a cringe, and claim me
dear.
But you only love me when you're drunk,
burps Jim.

The Robert with his long luscious hair all
shaved
mincing and moaning and feeling self-
conscious,
and Nellie neat who'll have a rum and
black
and demurely waits for the null of the
night.

Oh Royston, your vodka's spilt
          right down my sweater...
so it tingles her breasts as she says:
          Have a look?
Would you like her? You can have her?
          How much have you got?
Really! How could you?
          I have certain principles, you know!
Well, you can have her for those if you like.

There's Fred with her hair right down to
her waist
and smiling so weirdly and wan.
her skirt today was a table cloth once;
and, my dear, is it true you swim in the
nude?
How natural, how nasty, how brown you
are looking.

Yes, little Lordie, we've had a good time
and wrecked another dad's home.
When he returns he'll find beer on the
walls
and stains on the floor, the carpet and
beds.
We've all spent the night here, eight boys
and three girls,
and it's been pretty fair.

CHRISTMAS

You were once such a nice boy!
What I was once I'm not twice.

It's a Christmas he'll never forget,
For it's one he'll never remember.

Eve and in the afternoon
    snoring in an alley:
Wake up, sonny! What's your name?
    the bumptious lawman said.
Just call me Steve.

Money
    in his pockets
Meant
    for parents' presents,
Drinking
    in the public
With
    his present money.

A dreary drunken Christmas:
    a holiday from work,
    a generous season of the year –
    free cigarettes and beer –
    an excuse for special parties
    and kissing in the pubs,
    a carefree, reckless, mirthful time
    of complacent quick good will.
But, for Stephen with his charming grin,
    It's Christmas every day.

• • •

Blurred and pleasant
　　wrapped-up Christmas-present people

Old, and feeling
　　for the youth who's reeling homewards

Stare, and Stephen
　　stumbles to an even sweeter

Wine, and dinner
　　which awaits the sinner sleepy

After all his deeds,
　　doubtful how he succeeds to survive

A dreary drunken Christmas.

MUM SAID

He never talks
so how can I be expected to know
where's he's gone.
I often wish he'd tell me a few things
about his friends and his fun;
but no; he never talks.

He's out of work,
he's broken his apprenticeship you know,
and I think
he doesn't want to get another job,
his Dad has tried to help him;
but no, he's out of work.

He's never here,
except for meals which he eats three
hours late,
and at night,
although sometimes he's out until
morning.
We treat him well, it's his home;
but no, he's never here

JAZZ CLUB AGAIN

Through the nude show entrance, down
the cellar stairs,
    flash the pass then past the guard:
               and so? ...

Deep in the dark there's
the clarinet and casual crumpet,
    swaying and listlessly loving and jiving;
the long long hair and the long lost
clothes,
    the beards and the perhaps beards,
    the girls and the perhaps girls –
the darlings and the delights of the jazz-
notch gyp
    so vague an accepted and everything:
Sad and expressioned everything;
and nothing essential but this.

The little boy cute and loving and lucky,
    always got a girl and never ever
    something scruffy,
Scruffy! To some perhaps but to these
    it's real, it's theirs –
    this sad and sought seclusion.

Sad Cy's: merry in its melancholy,
    content with the crap of its kind:
Sad Cy's: the symbol of the
        someday-soon-but-not-just-yet:
Sad Cy's: so simple...
       and so bloody great.

MUM THINKS...

I gave the best years of my life for my son,
and suffered with thousands of others.
Amidst the shrapnel and shrieking
        and wailing of sirens
we managed to live.

And now from those months of weary
acceptance
and from those days of lightheaded
delusion,
has come a generation of children
        we don't understand
with memories of powdered eggs,
        powdered milk powdered bottoms
        and war.

I love you my son, though I don't get though
to express it
and you're nothing but a stranger to me.
But I pray that from my generation's
        mistakes
        you have learned
A way by which to save your poor children.

• • •

They never registered
for the National Service nonsense;
they didn't know
and, any way, couldn't be bothered.

But Jim wanted a break and was ready for
anything
so he quit his home and his girl
and signed on for twenty-one years.
Unenthusiastically he went
to fight as a paid paratrooper,
and he stuck to his stoic decision
with the bland and bored way of the clique.

One lost to the army because he's browned
off
Stephen thought that should have distressed
him:
His best friend has quit and is training to
kill,
while he is left learning to live.

LEARNING TO LIVE

Limp and blind with drink,
clinging, moaning,
      spewing
vaguely with a sigh:
and drawling irresponsibly
whilst flagging on his shoulders:
lurching with this bum
who's soberer than he
through the swaying nightmare streets
and fickle fields of slumber
to a home that's lost the way
which sprawling solid Stephen
mournful with a mood
of feeble fuddled splendour,
is searching with his mate
from a dear and sinking sleep
enticing him with bliss
throughout his drunken doze
casually in the rain
soaking in the street.

STEPHEN

Lend us a quid!
    I've signed at the dole office,
    but they're not paying me yet.
    You can have it as soon as I'm paid.

No, I won't!
    You must find some work,
    And I'll turn you out if you don't.

• • •

That girl he was with
    she's up the spout;
they tell me it's due in a few months.
You'd think he'd do something,
    at least get worried,
Yet he doesn't feel anything at all.

• • •

Vomit real and wretched
    writhing on the grass,
praying for the splutter to stop
    and ease his emptied guts;
yellow, green and moronic lumps
    of slimy stinking sick
pounding through his giddy head
    the shame of all his drinks.

• • •

Running out of splosh
         how about a ciggy,
The law's waiting for a chance,
         hold him for his cheek,
Cold and snidey snow,
         can't stay in bed all day,
Clique getting too well known,
         please find another pub,
His mate has got a steady,
         yank's meat but she's nice,
Moanings from his mum,
         why don't you get a job?

DISCOVERY

Take this guitar, kid,
let's see how you move –

Wow! What a boy!

Just sign up with Solly:
    you'll make lots of lolly
and find fame and thousands of fans –
isn't that what you want?

We'll cash in on your sadness,
    make something of your sweetness:
We'll call you Tavy Tender –
    you'll be the greatest teenage star.

TAVY TENDER

I never roll on the floor-
   pathos
   fire
   and sex appeal
I'm what every woman wants.

I wriggle with precision –
   power
   looks
and smouldering eyes
I thrill those whalebone judies.

They squeal at my name,
   they write on my car –
I've got what it takes
   to be a great star
   and knock up a thousand a week –
but I never, never roll on the floor.

• • •

No!... This is too big a future for Stephen –
   Perplexed and important
      He just wants to kip.

• • •

So
Slurring and snarling
   and wistfully pretty,
He mumbles and stumbles
   as he jives to gyp.

RAVE
1960

First published in May 1960 by the Scorpion Press with the note, "Acknowledgements are due to the editors of GEMINI in which the final poem in this book has already appeared.

For Tim The Merchant Sailor

Loving bold and be done with it –
          wash your hands afterwards, not
before;
dreaming brave and to hell with it –
          tossing and turning and kip where
you can:
shouting, spewing, drinking, moaning,
          from here to New Zealand –
          from port to clinic –
watching the waves of his wives

RAVE

*RAVE is a way of life. Julian and Sue are two
youngsters who are finding out about things. She
knows a bit more than he does and so they do not
stay together for very long. And then he starts to
find out more about living and is caught, when we
leave him, moaning about the cruel, hard, slot-
machined world. But he'll get used to it, just like
the rest of us.*

> *Royston Ellis,*
> *Brighton 1960.*

THIS IS JULIAN...

Slight and charming
with a curious flash of hair on his brow.

Small eyes gleaming
sadly at the others swaying with the
rhythm
from the juke box.

Softly talking
about his job as a bookie's runner
working for his father
living with his mother.

Sixteen tumbling years
playing shrew and cool
gazing through the haze
at the copper's nark.

• • •

Pass the cigarettes around Julian --
　　what! been turned out again?
You can kip down with me
old granny won't mind:
but watch out for her wooden leg –
　　it's hand carved!

COFFEE BAR

Couples crouched in a corner
and others sipping coke with ice.
By the juke box
a queer with a poodle called Lester.
At the counter
a chick with a bad reputation.

Grabbing the kids as they come through
the door
　　stands a man with thin paper tracts,
but we don't ride with religion
　　and men in thin plastic macks.

Sick of the gang living for kicks
the quick bird in the park,
the wild prowl through the night;
the restless depth of a lingering evening
sitting and waiting
　　for someone new to come in.

She's here every night
　　that old dear with her purse...

That old dear!
    Slender, *petite* I suppose they say,
    fawn costume, scarf round her head,
    silvery hair to her eyes
    and a cup of hot chocolate.

My name is Julian...
    Yes? I've just come from the cinema.
    Cars. They threw cars off a precipice
    and then a man threw his mother over,
    It was so real.

Do you live round here?
    In the black and white house
    that was ours
    until mother sold it.
    She sold the piano as well.

The little lady's lip quivered
    and her face glimmered
    with timid defiance.

    It was a boudoir grand,
    I don't know why she sold it,
    I always thought it was mine,
    now I can't play any more.

She looks about forty
    yet she's like a child.

    I don't work
    but I've tried,
    no one seems to want me to work...
    but I've tried.

Strange, very strange,
but at least she's a change from the
chicks.

We used to live in Hampstead
(she said as I walked her home)
in a house on a hill
with orange paint.

Come in and meet my mother's pug,
I don't understand it at all.

The dog sat on the sofa
on a leopard skin rug:
it panted and pawed
and giggled and roared
and snuffled a salivary hello.

The walls of the house
were hung with carpets and paintings,
thick curtains kept out the sun.
The rooms were rich
with rare antique furniture,
a warm musty smell,
and chips wrapped in *The Times* on the
table.

Then she showed me out
to latch the wrought iron gate...
and the house seemed like the rest in
the road.

THE LADS

Used to work on the buildings
    but the sun come out
    and well...so did we.

Used to be steady workers like
    before we went to pieces
    now we like to feel free.
We've got it all so easy now,
    our welfare and all that jazz:

    there's not much chance to feel free
    with politics, police and tax.

JESS

Jess is a good looking kid,
    a real ravin' dead beat lad,
We treat him like one of us
    but he's coloured.

We've heard of all the bundles
    and thuggery going on
But it never worries us
    that he's coloured.

Jess has fallen out with the law,
    he helped himself to a car,
but he needn't have tried to impress us
    'cause he's coloured.

UNCLE TRAMP

If you can't do the crime
   then don't do the time,
the man from the big house said,
   it's better this side of the water.

Scratching sodden and sacred in
the gutter
   and callously craving for snout
he should know, he's just walked from
Southampton
   where he did six months for intent.

You've got a kind face, sonny,
   will you give me sixpence for a cup of
tea?
I'll not do that, but I'll buy you a drink;
   so here's to the world, Uncle Tramp.

THIS IS SUE

Warm in the coffee bar gloom
   glinting with lunch time pleasure;
Snuggling tightly, lids sweetly closed,
   chuckling slightly, blatant repose:
She's on a ticking tacking spree
   with her tongue hanging out!

LUMBERING NOW

A glimpse from the flickering screen
   of a boy and his bird in the stalls –
   not cuddling and snogging
      right at the back
   but slumped in the front row
   sharing a basket of fruit.

   Sucking an orange with casual pleasure
   then munching an apple
   and punching his bird
   with warm understanding
   and a tender lack
   of any accepted traditions.

A long haired idle unbound boy
   and a glorious carefree maiden
   slumped in the front row of the stalls
   content with the mumbling harmony
   of their own idea of love.

        • • •

Those monumental ladies
   in pink and silver gowns,
   with airs of utter graciousness
   and breasts of classic firmness
   are not for him.

He likes a sluttish wench
   with no inhibitions
   or taste,
   just a cheeky skirt
   and a wilderness of hair...

She don't creach and scream
   like the marble girls
   at a party for launching the lads.
She's relaxed as she walks
   from one house to another
   just to scramble back into bed.

She's a sluttish wench
   with the urgent feeling
she's just got to live
like there's no tomorrow.

JULIAN

Easy, easy,
    break me in easy,

Sure I'm big time,
    cock-sure and brash,
but easy, easy,
    break me in easy.

Sure there've been others,
    I know the way,
but easy, easy,
break me in easy.

Let me hide,
    warm, deep and wet,
under the blanket
    and between your thighs

and easy, easy,
aaah – break me in easy.

SUE...

I remember last Summer,
that was the first time,
stretched taught on the beach
    with sand in my hair.

And then there was John,
    a sailor from faraway whores;
and Mick by the petrol pumps
    near Leicester Square.

And next blond William,
    for thirteen weeks,
with his warm brown body
    and holes in his socks.

But now it's tingling and take
    this shy little virgin
stabbing and stubbing and ...

aaah –I remember last Summer !

• • •

A red hot night
    of full blooded lust
is felt in the pain
at the pit of his stomach
with the ache and the twitch
in his oh-my-god thighs

JULIAN

I am a machine
   waking like a time
   from a dream.

   One two three
   rise and begin
   the shift –

   chug and stir
   and creak
   a clatter of cranking thought:

   essential – obliged -
   demand – emphatic -

   I am a machine
   waiting to be wound
   each day in despair...

   Oil the guts
   add fuel to the fingers
   and tighten the screw in the gullet.

I am an animal
   suddenly caught in a trap
   and frightened to snap at the bait.

   Wild and swift
   as the taut archer's arrow
   with the hiss of snake
   full of puss...

I am an animal
tame and serene
all pistons and buttons
just like a machine.

GROLLOPS

Saturday, saturday, saturday night
    down to the pub:

Cheers, my love. There's a right crowd
here tonight,
Are there any parties on, do you know?
All the boys have gone off to the toilet
where they'll take their time and frolic
like fools.
The drinks they are drinking at cruel and
confusing,
but blatant and bastard they'll writhe in
their pleasure.

A face like a bun all bloody and bloated
    splutters over its pint of bitter:
I've been here since six and I'm sixty-
seven.
    Really...

    The boys are back and the week's work
is being drunk.
George, a stout-and-cider, three browns
in their bottles,
a gin, a rum, a vodka-and-tonic,
and two of your pregnant pork pies – oh
cheers.
Now here's one for Sue. Have you got your
bag?
Am I a what?

Saturday, saturday, saturday night
    along to the party:

How young are you, old timer?
   brushing your beard and brooding.
As young as you're not.

Well, behave yourself tonight, darling,
   try not to spew on the trifle,
and if you must go upstairs with a woman
   please find one I wasn't at school with.

So grasping his moustache
   he led himself out
   by his whiskers and wondering wife.

• • •

Ribbons, ribs, and carpet
   and grollops grieving in curly pairs.
   There's Sue, so tipsy, tired,
     and terribly tight
   with a scoreboard on her panties.

• • •

Mother...this is Davy's hanky:
   it's bloody 'cause he cut his finger
   lifting up a drain
     to fish for Julian's lost
cigarettes.

Sailing down a sewer in a bandy boat of
bed clothes,
waving Davy's hanky and searching for
Julian's fags –
sailing out to sea on a sackcloth made of
sawdust
and tippling all the council men

with lovers stuck on poles.

There's pied piper Neptune
   in grey striped jeans
(so dirty and sexy in his nice clean sewer)
ruthlessly wading and wielding his
office.
and pulling the chain of his
   plastic pink toll gate
as he demands a light for Julian's
   lost cigarettes.

• • •

Now ...
   how young are you old timer?
      brushing your beard
        and brooding.
   Older than the last time – Sir!

• • •

He looks into his eyes –
   surely something must show?
but no, they are still young.

He reasons with his mind –
   no doubts? no passion?
but his sneer is hard and practical.

He listens for a shout –
   won't they see him going out?
but he hears the early morning wind
and the seagulls crying out.

• • •

Julian,
think of your chick.
   Huh huh.

What's she like?
   All right.

Got a good figure?
   Umm.

Why do you chat her then?
   Thighs.

   Oooh-ah thighs
      just for me
      (Oh yes?)
   Aaah-oh thighs,
      thighs of my dreams

Where is she tonight?
   Dunno.

Do you want another drink?
   Ummmmmmmmmm!

· · ·

Rave
   and swirl
on a moody pattern
that beats out a drum
that must have soul
jabbed with relish
and laughter
streaming down a cheek
and swirling hair

raving –
shimmering –
glistening –
throbbing –
dancing faster
round the floor
under the table and on to the bed
heaving and grinning and dying...

and the milkman's round early this
morning.

• • •

It's Monday morning,
    Monday,
It's time for work.

He drags himself out of bed
    wash
        breakfast
walking down the road to work.
Going to be late
    so!
there's the gate
    clock in.

Go to the bench
    start the press
    run through the steam
    set off the catch
    fix the furnace
and wait at the cooler.

Here's the foreman

the big barrel of
    hate him
You was late
   don't do it again.
Kick and curse the conveyor belt.

Tea break
   what a drag
   another eight hours
   and then knock off.

Back to the press
   with its shudders
     and grease
   and faultless performance.

You've not got enough steam,
   that fine figure of a foreman,
Wake yourself up, lad.

That's it,
   that's just it,
Jacking.
Keep your lousy job.

It's Monday morning,
   Monday,
walking up the road out of work.

• • •

When I die
   don't bury me here –
just cut up my bones
   and give them to the dogs.

Tell them this
   as they snarl and gnaw
that I turned my back
   on the wind and the rain.

My back was broad
   and my life was short
but to hell with them all
   that smothered my breath

for here was a yearning
   and a desperate attempt
but they were there first
   with their sickening decrees.

So I turned my back
   on the wind and the rain –
now cut up my bones
   and give them to the dogs.

• • •

He sits in the dark
one hand on his crutch
the other fiddling with a fag packet.

• • •

I saw Sue again last night.

So what?
   I don't sleep with her any more, you
know.
   I sleep with my cat.

It – poor thing – jumps through the

window onto the bed
    and purrs
    at my snores
    as it snuggles
    triumphantly under the blankets.

It licks
with its tongue
scraping my chin
and shivering into my slumber.

I turn
and mutter in vain –
it just lies on my head
and blinks itself slyly to sleep.

I could kill that cat
    Bit I'm always too tuckin tired.

• • •

Shatter this gentle daze.
    How cruel!

Turn on the taps and drown the spider
    with
Water rushing down a shoot,
    lilies on my grave,
Carry me from this sickly place
    and bathe my wound in beer.

Dance a merrydown roundelay
    and tumble with succulent kisses.
The fire is out in the hearth
    yet my sword is carving deep.

Now skip along my little one,
     lilies at your birth,
Straight and sturdy as the day
     Bids arrows flecked with pain.

Be lulled once more by rippling sounds
     mellow now in agony,
And bear your ancient shield of gold
     to new weapons dipped in blood.

• • •

I have seen your river banks
     with drainage, flies and fishermen;
And I have followed your quaint canal
paths
     through factories, fields and building
projects.

I have climbed your trees
     and walked along your country lanes;
I have seen your bottles and envelopes of
lust
     and your filthy rags which blossom on
the hedgerows.

I have called up your cattle at dawn
     and sipped your fresh-teated milk;
And I have cut your corn in the sweltering
sun
     and eaten your bleached, synthetic
bread.

I have put flowers in a vase on a grave
     and read of your bombs and your
power;

I have been to your smart new towns
     and seen your smart new people, now
equal to all.

I have roamed around your motherland
     with her kindness and slyness profuse;
And I have raved on with the rest
     at your heroes, homes and neat little
jobs.

I have lived your life
     and know the sorrows you must bear;
And now I am dying your death
     with my head, my soul, and my sins –

     and your worms nibbling my delicate
fingers.

THE RAINBOW WALKING STICK
1961

*To commemorate his twentieth birthday
on February 10, 1961, and the attainment
of middle age, ROYSTON ELLIS respectfully
dedicates this pamphlet to the friends
of his teenage years.*

*Printed for the author by Weekly Post
Newspapers Ltd. Distributed for him by
Scorpion Press, 11, Rofant Road,
Northword, Middlesex, at 6d per copy in 1961*

For all those quick pretenders
Who strutted through the past
Leaving dew-wet flowers as
blossoms on the mattress

RAINBOW WALKING STICK

Come, gently now,
Take my hand,
Over the mountain
To Lagric's land.

Tucked in a valley
On Drainpipe wood,
Over the slag heap
Where Sarah once stood

Her eyes on the town:
Narrow streets, black smoke,
Factory hooters, tall chimneys
Belching filth. Choke

Cough, splutter;
The houses creak
As the earth subsides a fraction per week.

Home is a jar
Of industrial sweat,
Each adult a slave,
Each day a threat

Of the gloom in the pit,
The clock at the gate,
The foreman's whistle,
The sack for being late.

For the festering grind
Stockily stands
Like pillar and tether
For a boy with two hands.

Days bled at a desk,
At a bench, on a site;
Evenings, unshackled!
Freedom flows through the night.

Come gently now
Split from the scene
Out of the parlour
Into the green

Beyond the ridge
Of pre-cast sludge
Bounding the town
Of industrial drudge.

Shout goodbye
To Mum stretched at the sink.
Then make for the track
That leads where you think.

Over the heap
Where Sarah once stood
out of that jail
To Drainpipe wood

Hack through the weeds
Kick past the cans
crawl under the thatch
Then stand...
At the edge of the glade
Which is Beer Bottle Patch.

THE MATTRESS FLOWERS

A flower
Slender struggling stem
With ripples of green
Fly and carefree,
Grows on a mattress
On semen of centuries,
The mire of mysteries
and drunken romping
Spread by the blossom of impropriety,
And flourishes
As the fragile bud shyly reaches
From kapok for succour from sun
And just a drench from dew and rain
Bursting magnificent breeze-weaving
beauty
Petals of pink and stamen of yellow;
Blushed by oaths of council men
Tipping gas stoves, cartons, tins and taps,
Sacks, oil drums and paper hats,
On a crawling fox, car doors and coats
Decaying at the bottom of the pit
Scented by urine and burdock
And cows in the field beyond the ridge of
trees
Branches trailing with warm tea-leaves
Tumbled and sloshed by automatic
women
From grimy urn into factory dustbin:
This to fertilize the mattress flower,
A graceful prize, a pride through climax
Destined, discarded loves and lives
Dumped stinking by revellers
on Beer Bottle Patch.

ROUSE, FIZZLE & PLOP

No one is to blame.
The newspapers were rustling to work
When I saw
The one-arm bandit wheeled up Wardour
Street.

Someone spoke. He was
A seraphic sort of fellow blotched by gnat
bites.
Clean as a queer.

Intercourse it!
    I beg your pardon?
This lousy burg's a lousy morgue.
    No doubt you are right.
    Platonic warfare every time.

This is the end, cruel world – I'm flushed!
And with that he gurgled away.
But what else could I do?

ACHING SPRING

It was a morning chill that, roused by rain
    Hammering down howling streets
    Cars rattling over cobbled women
Shrieking with delighted tuts
And moans from aching springs which
pang
    Stuck with husbands paunch and limp
    Frolicking beds that drip to propping
bars
Stirred by an easy couple clasped and
romping
    Through the retired and hankering
town,
    Wakened sighs from forgotten leaps
When lithe the wind stopped throbbing
the lair
    And prickle-closed lid eyed pots
    And kettles hissing gossip;
Hot gin in knobbly stone bottles slid
    To breathe warm air into clamouring
sheets
    Stuck like friends together
Wiping steam from the grip
    of the morning chill.

• • •

Straight tears of taut temptation
    Like a warm trickle of weary disgust,
Whelp and flow for an old man's sorrow
    And his struggle to tumble tonight.

A smiling creature smelling sweet
    Shouting and strutting so young

Was a whisper of some secret wish
   To an old man's mind torn by time.

The unformed face with a lifetime left
   Of a quivering vision so pure
Haunts the weathered dreams of an old
man dying
   With a blaze of blood on his brow.

THE RAINBOW WALKING-STICK

Clutch at a rainbow walking stick
Now that wobbling shadows throb thick
And stumbling desire gropes sprawled
In heaving mud, legs clawed
And tight entwined with pressure
Panting, and surprised as pleasure
Leaps...and glimmers...and dies
Thrust through by fear of eyes
Lurking like bawling aldermen
Behind flame pillars of adult men.

Their tags destroy any innocence
Wrought splendid once in silence
Now tattered by tongues hissing talk.
Warped by their duties, they lark
As middle age creeps like spunk on a
sponge
Into body-washed brains.
But seeds of children lunge
And bloom out of their envy
Into life.

Lest those future years in a shroud
suffocate
Lean for strength on your rainbow
walking stick.

AS THE ANGEL FLIES

Chatter, each finger wagging
brown sweat and sniff, and chant
your triumphs, eager being;
body built to plunge and snarl
tight face, hard eyes, and viciousness
grinding to exhaustion.

Blood bursts upon your satisfaction
and phlegm flows round the blanket lair.

The lover blinks as the angel flees
like a whore from a hermit's nest.

THE BURN UP
1962

Originally performed to music composed by
Humphrey Searle and spoken by Denys
Hawthorne at Hamptons & Teddington Music
Club Musica Viva, St James Square, London
24 February 1962

Fine Arts Chamber Group
Yyrah Norman (violin); Harold Harriott (viola);
Eleanor Warren ('cello); Thea King (clarinet);
Peter Wallfisch (piano); with James Blades
(Percussion); John Leach (Cimbalom).

THE BURN UP

It was warm inside
The glittering glass cage beside
The hurtling by-pass rumbling to town
Drivers passing, or pulling in to unwind
At the tables, and stretch weary limbs
Twitched to tap to the beat from the juke
box.

It was cold outside
And lonely, but the boy astride
The huge trembling machine, was
swathed
In metal and leather, sheltered by the
dark
Endless hulks of aching lorries
Creaking with loads bounced
From the Midlands.

Alone
In an individual huddle
Ticking over his thoughts
As gasps of egg and bacon
And truckers' chatter
Wafted around him
As the door opened and shut.

Aloof
And unimpressed by others
Silent and throbbing
With the machine beneath him
Waiting for more bikes and riders
To roar in off the road
And swop some technical detail.

Cranking in the pots
Whisker in the carb
Tanking it at eighty
Hammering with the ton.

Inside
The transport café
Smudged drivers eat their grub;
A letter stuck by the till
Written with weak shaking hand
Is from a forgotten boy's mum:
Thanks for the wreath you sent for my son.

A streak
Cracks past the car park,
Rider crouched low over machine
Chasing the curves of the road.
The boy outside the café stirs,
Throttles his bike to life;
Trembling with the eager rhythm
He jerks his legs like props from the
ground
Tucks them on rests to tickle controls
And eases his bike with a gentle grunt
Out of the pull-in onto the rattling
highway.

Waiting a break in the chain of headlights
Jogging with loads and sleepy passengers:
Boy and bike, alert and straining.
Slack right hand grips and twists,
Bones tightening with anticipation
Underneath black leather glove,
The revolving end of the handlebar;
Right leg shifts in a secret pattern,

Sensitive foot in a black leather boot
Taps a latch for gear;
Clasped left hand relaxes grip
Unfolding in rigid time the clutch;
Right hand's finger let's slip the brake;
Left leg up and release the wheel:
Split second bang, boy and bike as one
With a clout of power in a gap
Zip across the road and away.

Rush of wind
Biting into flesh of face
Left uncovered by scarf, and mouth,
Goggles at eyes,
Encased in crash helmet
With spaceman shape,
Century's eccentric symbol.
Speed of spaceman
As right leg taps the pattern
Left hand playing clutch
Building greater power,
Thrust from deeper booster
Somewhere sunk in thighs
Hugging super-charged steel structure
Calmly hurtling at breath-take break-
neck speed
Out of this world
Along the M-One.

Lunging past the grumbling tankers,
Drivers spitting out his fate,
Weaving past the straining family seaters,
Mothers gape in startled fear,
Pulling away from the chain of traffic
Into streaks of unravelling night
Tugging past his howling ear

With the blaze of a roaring demon
Driving through a stretch of road his own.

The ground beneath him whistling away;
The strength in his bike to conquer the
world,
A king speeding along without any shame.
A man free and proud, as a boy should be.

A flash of tree,
An endless switchback line of fields.
A distant blur of a sudden house;
A reckless riotous
Vibrant boy
Living living living ...

What's that?
In the shadows ahead!
Too late...
Another beam begins to stab
And carve a path.
First a prick
Now growing bigger;
An inverted arrow of light
Spreading through the stretch of darkness
Outlined by crouching low on machine.

A glance behind
Ah there he is
On a six-fifty-twin,
Johnny out for kicks again.

Slow down,
Tease him;
Coax him up, then hammer away.

Growing blaze creeps closer,
Engine revving viciously;
Boy gaining...
Ready!

Two bikes growling together
Poised
Right hands quivering
Throttles avid
Poised at forty
Poised at fifty
Poised at fifty-five ...
Burn up!

Crouched low
Eyes on the road
Eyes out of the corner
On each other
Trottles opening faster
Faster
Needles touching sixty
Seventy
Eighty.

Wind prising
Power gripping
Banging body forward.
Throat tightening
Climax rising
Neither gaining
Bikes together
Desperate
Desperate
Tank it further
Faster
Faster

Ninety,
One,
Two,
Three,
Four,
Five,
Six, seven.

Got to beat him
More
More
Oh make it faster
Where's that speed!
Burn-up, burn-up burn-up
Faster
Touched the ton,
Ton-ten perhaps.

He's slipping.

Hedges, houses, ditches, fences
Lanes, lines, signs and senses,
Flashing in the urge to burn …

He's slipped, dropped back,
Other beaten!
Burn up won!
Rape the road
And bellow at the conquest …
Boy and bike become at speed.

Gently ease it off,
Proved his point,
Glistening with exhilaration.
Slowing down –
A mere eighty now –

Two bikes growling together.
A flush and a grin,
Wind whips at speed
Warmth within
Under leather and metal,
Racing through the night;
Legs playing the pattern,
Cogs spinning,
Changing down,
Dropping slower
Out of the highway,
Laying close to the ground
Round a bend,
Scraping footrests
Scattering merry fireworks.

A mile ahead
Another café glare,
Drop a gear,
Swerve in
Behind the aching hulks
Of long long-distance lorries
To a pack of rugged angels
Standing exclusively with slow jealous
pride
Round a string of bristling machines
Two boys and bikes together
Drop in out of the night
At the end of a burn up.

BERLIN, 1962

BERLIN BAR

(Written in January 1962;
previously unpublished)

Under a table in the Eve Bar, Berlin,
Lies a drunken soldier from the Durham
Light.
Two others, slumped across two tarts. Shout
For the waiter to bring five cognacs.

Outside, the wide street waits,
Trams clattering, neon signs glittering,
For the dawn to grip
The nightly revellers struggling home
Through the deserted coach terminus
And up the steps to Charlottenburg Sta-
tion.

Two grey-blue police with pistols and
sticks
Watch from a corner as a British soldier
Buys a curried sausage
And drops it on the floor.

Night: six streets away from the Eastern
Zone
In the British controlled Soho of West
Berlin
In Kaiser-Friedrickstrasse
Between bars, behinds clusters of boys,
Is the frantic glimmer of a nervous home
For the city's restless population;
Through the tingling darkness, the Eve
Bar quivers.

Two waiters on a twelve-hour shift
Waft through the night prodding sleepers
And bullying drinkers to order more,
Fetching concoctions from the tapster
Driving a chrome-plated beer machine
Watched by a dark-suited gentleman
Who takes the money.
Two girls behind the counter smiling
Wondering where they'll sleep in the
morning.

At the juke box, a crack from the beat
Whips jivers in the crowd in a hot German
stomp,
Long hair fluttering and breasts rolling
With rhythm. Music pounds throughout
this city
Where angry urges are lashed by pleasure
In this fading ever-open teenage bar.

A group of sturdy Aryan youngsters
Bang down their glasses; quick eyes
Seeing all that happens as
They doodle swastikas in pools of beer
And, chewing gum, worship Hitler.
In a corner a boy whimpers,
His throat and wrists slashed in a fight.
The blood drips onto his black leather
jacket
As his girl drags him away to hide in her
room.

Do you want the toilet? Down there on
the right.
Gruff Mickey in white coat and jeans
Points to a trough in a backroom cupboard,

Blocking the entrance: Ten pfennigs
please.
What for? For the toilet; I keep it clean.
I want to eat and get my clothes from the
laundry.
I'm an orphan and only Big Effie loves me.

Big Effie sits in the arms of a soldier
Halting his hands with a weary smile:
Twenty marks for her, eight marks eighty
the room.
He haggles in vain then winks at his mate
And goes for half-an-hour of Big Effie's
short time.

The girls chat the men who've dropped
out of the world
To this festering den of boys and unli-
censed whores;
Lost and frightened, the men need to buy
friends
For comfort and strength to lift their despair.

You look very lonely, boy. That's not good.
A man feels her talk though the heavy
dark air
And turns as her words breathe into his
ear.
It's bad to be sad at this time of night.
That's okay. Like a drink?
On no thanks! She sits at the table and
waits.
Please have one, it's all right.
Well, a blue milk and ice would be nice.

The man brings out his wallet and orders
The first round that will get him the girl
And ruin his night; because
Unless his fingers catch the Eve Bar pulse
He is destined to throb all alone.

Another three rounds, his hand on her
knees
Instead, she ignores his passionate pleas
And talks about the weather, signalling
Mickey.
Do you mind if I join you? Oh please.
This is Mickey, my cousin, won't you buy
him a drink?
Sure, sure.

The old routine. The stranger's new
friends
Are like a brother and sister to him.
He's happy in his stupor, as other fingers
creep
To empty his wallet.
Mickey and the girl drift silently away.

Pouring cognac from a frozen bottle
With a hidden grin, the blond young tapster keeping eager watch on the Eve Bar
orphans
Thinking of his cut tomorrow.

Seeing I've caught his thoughts, he turns
To pack a crate of cokes in the fridge.

A few minutes pass, the riot continues,
The tapster dispensing glasses of foam
with beer.

Lines of doubt streak across his youthful
face
Then vanish.
I've seen you in here
Before.
You sat at the counter last night.

The words knocked me out of my mood.
Is Mickey your friend? Yes, we crossed
Over the border together. It was
Early August then, when refugees
swarmed
With ease to the west by road, bus and
s-bahn.

I was a locksmith, training, slaving for
Ulbricht
Now I'm free to do what I like.

Morning slowly seeps into sight
Stirring newspaper huts and fruit barrows
At the corners of the streets into life
As tired ghosts peer out of the cellars
To feel their way home or float back to the
counters.

Klaus, the tapster, beer-pulling done for
the night
Pulls on a jerkin over his bare-chested
shirt
And comes around the counter to hug me.

Into Friedrichstrasse, eyes hooded
To filter the day's vicious glare
And reel like idiot chickens, necks wrung,
From a roost to the East by overground
train

We stumble up to the blue-uniformed
crone
Wedged into her ticket office knitting.
Two to Alexander Platz. Please.

At the barrier a lazy guard
Clips the tickets then watches as
We run up the steps and leap into
A rattling, tram-like train. It is
A sturdy wooden box with windows
And narrow wooden seats, self-opening
doors
And complicated maps of coloured routes
Sprawled like a psychologist's test:
The links joining split Berlin.

There's the memorial, that slab erection
With concrete fingers pointing to the sky.
See that curved roof, saucer-like on pillars,
The concert hall in sheer magnificence.
That glint over there is the eagle catching
the sun.
Down that street at the end is the Bran-
denburger Tor.

The overhead railway skims like a low-
flying plane
Through a city of saloons and monuments.

The last station in the West. No one's get-
ting off.
The train pulls away and curves over a
canal.
Here we are in the Russian Zone, East
Berlin.

Klaus has fallen asleep, his head slumped
On my shoulder, or is he acting
Fear twisting his nerves to breaking
Point.
He snores
A couple of guards on the platform
A lot of women with worn out shopping
bags
A nasty little man who must be a spy
A boy with a toy gun, a baby crying;
The same scene anywhere. The train clat-
ters on
Deep into the red sector, a foreign land
Riddled with excitement for a stranger
like me,
A boring journey for Klaus, once his home
Now a bit of his past before he became
An Eve Bar orphan.

Alexander Platz! We walk with his secret
Into the foreboding alien street, and see
Three American tourists with movie cam-
eras,
Two Chinese gentlemen chattering,
And an optician from Sheffield out with
his wife
Sight-seeing.

We left the grim silence of the east,
His memories of childhood;
His fleeing from home and hard work
Disturbed him; the torn roots
Of life were tingling too much.
But that night, back in the Eve Bar,
Watching behind his machine

The glitter, the gloom, his own Berlin
He felt secure again.

S-BAHN, BERLIN

(January 1962)

Zoo Station, a bright world, clean,
Glittering windows, buildings and people
stretching upwards.
Twenty West pffenigs, a red-printed card
Clipped with boredom by a fat collector
Squeezed, bosom overhanging, in her
sentinel box.

Race up wide stairs to the fatal platform.

Friedrichstrasse blazes from the indica-
tor,
A railway guard in peak cap drinks at the
bar;
Three Chinese tourists jabber together
As he stands, amused by the news, on his
journey again.

The train to the East bangs in.

Pull open the doors then sit in a slight
sweat
On wooden seats on the right hand side
To look out of the window as the train
curves round
After two more stops into the forbidden
land.

At the end of that street
They've bricked up the Brandenburg
Gate.

Three blue-uniformed police guards
stand at the bridge
Whilst the train clinks past them over the
canal.
One peers through binoculars at a clump
of trees,
The others idly fondle highly-polished
machine guns.

Behind, in the West, a stars-and-stripes
flutters.

The train weaves to a halt at Friedrichstrasse;
Mouth dry, hands sticky, he strides unper-
turbed
Past more railway guards, colts at their
hips,
Down wide stairs to the police at the bottom.

They glance at his passport and point to
the customs.

At the makeshift counter stand three
grey-uniformed men,
Prodding and probing the latest arrivals.
Tourist, he lies blandly. Such a fuss. No
cash, nothing!
They smile and wave the mad Englander
through.

Herr Ulbricht's wall underground blocks
the way to the street.

More blue-uniformed guards, all blond
sturdy men,

Crowd around to examine credentials.
They peer at his, find an out-of-date Rus-
sian visa,
And let him step through to the ruin of
East Berlin.

Here is a crumbling Midland's town
Without many people.

A policeman in green carrying a case
walks past,
Two workers with rifles stand guard on a
tank,
Three Russian soldiers in brown zoom by
in a jeep.

Quickly round the station to a different
entrance;
Twenty East pffenigs, a black-printed card
Clipped with boredom by a fat collector
Squeezed, bosom overhanging, into her
sentinel box.

A train clatters to another station,
To the heart of people trapped
Behind the brick wall.

A hundred tipped cigarettes, half-a-kilo
of coffee,
A block of milk chocolate, Ost-Marks from
the West
For secret friends. They give in exchange
Letters, love and thanks
To the brothers and neighbours who
escaped.

JOURNEY

(February 1962)

There are Polish students buying beer
In the buffet at Warsaw station, squat
glasses
And heads tossed back in a native toast.
In the street a strawberry cart clatters
Over busy tram lines. A fat woman in rags
Waves a stick and shrieks at her donkey.
An Italian boy-jockey shakes my hand
And next day I'm in a garland.

Under the table in the Eve Bar, Berlin,
At home at last in Big Effie's arms.
Over the roof tops by S-bahn lives my
brother,
A dustman behind Herr Ulbricht's wall
Reaping the benefits of being a good hus-
band
In a relentless city; and Hajo in the Eve
Bar
Earns for his lost beauty and Big Effie
Who sleeps in the cellar with Mickey.
Klaus twinkles cognac into my glass
As I think of Yevgeni in Moscow.

The teenage hero, he waved a fistful of
roubles
And dismissed our farewell dinner;
My forgotten treasured drummer gleamed
Like a child who still knows life is good.
Some days later I sailed into Copenhagen
And slept on the beach by the brewery.

Now it is winter and I know I've never
been
Anywhere at all; it was just a dream
Of a summer's night when the world
turned
And the tide washed me up on the shore.

For Yevgeni Yevtushenko

I flew
Over two hundred kilometres
From my father's home on a tiny island
To be with you again
When you were in London.

I saw
You at a reception for clever people;
Famous writers, painters and name-
dropping snobs
Who crowded round to touch you.

Our eyes
Met suddenly and in our hearts
We renewed our Moscow friendship
When we were two
Poets linked by the message of youth
Understood
Secrets politicians never heard.

Alas,
Those people around you
Were like moths blotting out the light
Which attracts them.
We could not speak
Instead, in despair, I drank the vodka
Provided by the British Council, your
hosts,
And passed out.

THE RUGGED ANGEL, 1962-63

(previously unpublished)

For Golden John

(i)

Outside the all night transport café
Cars and lorries line the pull-in
Like mechanical shadows in love.

A headlight beam swings off the road,
Twists, pokes, and glides to park,
And picks out of the night a boy in a car.

He sits straight up, blond hair on his brow,
His eyes probably closed in sleep
Behind the mysterious squares of cheap
sunglasses.

His face is young, his body slight,
And a quiver of laughter taunts his lips;

No furrows tremble, lurking to scar
The beautiful face of a being scarcely begun
On a journey from past to future.

Perhaps he's a musician returning from play,
Perhaps he's an angel dropped in for the
night;
Or perhaps he's trade, this boy in a car.

(ii)

The boy in the car gets out, shouts his thanks
At the anonymous driver in the white con-
vertible
As it leaps away into the rest of the night.

He stands, eyes confidently surveying the
streets
Of the lonely suburb he has inevitably
reached,
Knowing within minutes he will find the action
That irks the respectable chill of this out-
skirts station.

A skip in the shadows, a strut of delight
For incredible adventures he knows are to
come
According to the whims of his mischievous
good luck.

He tilts back his head, listens to the night
As though he can hear the throbbing heart-
beat
Of the lace-curtained semi-detached street
Already half-asleep; but he hears the music
Of youth's bold laughter on top of the world
In a corner pub several blocks away.

Poised like a runner tensed for the gun,
Like a masochistic cat chattering a yard
from its prey,
Like an unknown angel about to descend
Out of the dark sky to an unknown land,
He sighs and lets slip an intriguing smile.

In the depths of the corner pub, a lull
Overtakes the general conversation
And stops it, as the authorities
With beards, striped shirts and French
cigarettes
Pause to sip at their pints; as the young men
Impatient, fidgeting, blinking and
calculating,
Concentrate; as the barman pouring Scotch,
Wiping glasses, chatting customers,
mopping counters
Counting change, eases up to rest his feet;
The door opens and the boy slips into their
lives.

All eyes in their various ways take in
His black leather jacket glistening with dew,
His faded levis, tempered in oil, and
bunched
Beneath his buckled belt, his black leather
boots;
His careless eyes, his lingering lips,
As he casually fingers his hips.

That night I took him back for coffee and
asked:
What time shall I set the alarm for?

(iii)

The door through a wall reveals a secret
Of the summer when the angel was born:

Push it open to see half naked a figure
Flaked out in the sun, his arms stretched
Above his head, palms open, fingers wide,
In a forgotten garden where wild flowers
bloom
And he, liked the flowers picked to adorn
The dining table, the lounge; a touch of
nature;
Is plucked by grasping hands beyond the
wall
To stand, his father's representative,
In the festering lounge of your life.

(iv)

This stark naked stranger sleeps beside me:

I sense the warmth from a young body
Swelling through my private sheets to pause
Where ultimate decision flows.

It is a body lingering on the tip of a dream:
Dark hair over soft-closed eyes, a smile
Twitching vaguely – a rich mouth
Where kisses blossom; sudden jerk of leg
Before a confident sigh stirs an uncompli-
cated face.

I fill with thoughts, rouse with love
And twist with frantic memory,
In the brutal light of a grey tasting dawn
Of the fantastic night a thousand years be-
fore
When the rugged angel came to my bed.
I turn to grip that young body now
As that warmth and my sudden knowledge
Help me see my stranger better.

(v)

You met me on the ferry.
I was a deck boy, and you were a passenger.
I called you "Sir."

Then I lost my job and came to you
Because I was broke and needed help.
You took me for yourself for a night.
In the morning I left for Southampton
With money I think I had earned.

Then I came to you a second time
To beg my fare home to Belfast.
I swore I would repay every penny,
I suppose I meant it, and you said you
would wait
For the pleasure or payment you hoped
in return.

Then I left and haven't come back.
You think I have lost a friend?
Now remember, I called you "Sir."

(vi)

The boy bent over the bar billiard table,
Cue in hand, positions for a shot and sees
With a glance from uplifted eyes
A figure he knows too well.
He pots the ball and continues the game.

A crowded bar, all types, so no one notices
The old colonel, brisk chipped moustache,
Red face, white hair, blue regiment tie,
Stride eagerly in, puffing a Havana cigar.
The boy pots the ball and continues the
game.

The colonel speaks, the boy replies,
And the military shadow retreats from the
bar
As the boy pots the ball and finishes the
game.
Suede jacket in hand, comb through blond
hair,
He slips ten minutes later into the night
And a car round the corner to the colonel's
estate.

A private affair for the colonel in bed
Labouring beneath his plump shell of ar-
mour
To pierce the enemy lines drawn up
In a bare-faced arc, knees to chin,
Cheek, cheek, and red-creased lips.
Charge! roars the colonel's battle ardour
But none of his subaltern's vigour seeps
through.

Damn! puffs the old warrior with wrinkled
despair;
Try another night, less Scotch, more fire.
Now it's rent for the boy, wearied dreams for
the man
And a time for them both when the end will
come.

(vii)

He bends down, his long black hair
Flowing down to teenage shoulders as he
pulls
Off his socks and sits
On the edge of the bed;
He pulls and he is naked
In front of him, his schoolboy prefect
His naked virgin, standing before him;
perfect,
Proud of his unspoilt body
And proud of him, his young slave.

He has come to him from a man
He met last night in the pub
And slept with.
A simple lust up for cash as they mingled
With riotous delight at solid sex
twice before they fell asleep
And once again this morning.
His body paid for at his disposal.

He is his virgin, his tender body
Stretched out, new born, baby pure,
Pounding against his; his hands marvelling
At the creature lying with him;
His boy, and the boy who goes with anyone.

He wants me to taste him inside me,
To know that beauty I have yet to feel,
To be his because he loves me.
But, like children, we play in innocence
And with the afternoon sun through the
curtains

Warming his buttocks close to me,
He makes love to my navel.

They fall asleep in each other's arms
For a couple of hours then he leaves until
tomorrow
To hunt the colonel who'll take him
And make him a man again, not a schoolboy's
lover.

(viii)

He leaps out of bed and stands
Naked before my mirror, a long mirror
In which he can see all of himself, as he
wonders
What love has done to his angelic form.

He sees the lithe brown shape of summer,
The strong proud muscles of winter
The healthy fire of a young man
With pleasure alive in his limbs.

He turns round and peers over his shoulder
At the beautiful curve of a perfect halo
And the grace of his motorbike thighs.
He smiles, picks up my wallet and sighs.

(ix)

I want to treasure every stain on that sheet.
Is that one of his hairs? No nugget?
(The gold as he slipped in bed beside
And kissed my body, soon to be his.)
That sheet held up to the sunlight
Shows, yes, Christ! glorious dimples
And little maps of Australia.
I'll sleep in his body print tonight.

(x)

Stalking through evening streets
A stirring silhouette, a soaring creature,
An indescribable ache-in-the-stomach
attraction,
Ignoring the frantic search of empty pre-bed
hours
Knowing soon his immediate appeal
Will snare a yearning body
To excite, have ... discard;
He, at the flash of his vanity, sighs
For release, discharge
From that underhang of automatic lust,
That plastic scrotum dispensing instant
potence
In mockery, memory and savage working
order
As each nightly pounding toughened his
pestle
An instrument now too hard to regret
Losing the sensitive innocence of love.

(xi)

He parks the stolen bike at the harbour's
edge to stand
with legs apart at the edge of the quay
where tires bob on a chain and birds smell
of the sea
as they shout about their freedom. A hand
tugs
his shoulder and he turns from
contemplating the clinging barnacles
on the granite slabs of perpetual harbour
wall
to look across where little boats
wait for their weekend owners. He shrugs.
The winter sun shines down on his halo of
golden hair;
A black oil skin, a duffle bag, face to dare;
wreathed in thought, eyes mild, mind wild;
Not just for a journey to another place
But for the next voyage in this rugged angel's
life.

The boat draws alongside to take him across
the water.

THE SEAMAN'S SUITCASE

THE SEAMAN'S SUITCASE
To commmorate being registered
as a boat engineer, States of Guernsey,
Channel Islands, 1963,
the author respectfully dedicates
these poems to Tony & Jet,
Christine Keeller; and The Beatles
in admiration of their achievements.

Printed for the author by Weekly Post
Newspapers Ltd. Price 6d per copy.

THE SEAMAN'S SUITCASE

(1)

Behind him
a battered black suitcase in a bedroom;
a lodger fled, a jumble of belongings
to sort through and to recover the rent.
The lid flicks back and a smell of sweat,
of a seaman's travels, of brothels, of beer,
fills the landlady's neat room on the
waterfront.
In faint chalk on the lid "Go Home Yank"
stares
as tired hands turn back a blue seaman's
Guernsey
to rummage through two pairs of suede
shoes
and a find a bright green shirt, a Lybro
jacket,
and a Christmas menu from the *Rangitoto*.
A screwed up dirty handkerchief nestles
on the brim of a greasy French fisherman's
cap;
underneath, a pair of swimming trunks
with a plastic anchor sown on the pouch.
There's a synthetic-leather brush and comb
set,
a forgotten present from a loving aunt,
and a pair of light blue, thick cotton vests
which, cut up, will make good dusters.
The American nude book with eager women
in plastic macks and kinky positions

is exchangeable at a shop in Kentish Town;
there's a card from a bar in South Carolina
and a poem clipped from an Aussie mag
about a busty girl on an escalator.
Under a stiff white collar turning yellow
lies a cigar box bought in Amsterdam
filled with sad envelopes labelled "Assorted"
                    and "Self."
A jazz band in Copenhagen, a Jamaican view,
the New York skyline, Pitcairn Island canoes;
snaps of shores where this young seaman
raved.
Photos of ports, homes, girls and ships;
youths in St Christophers, bronzed muscles
flexed,
eyes laughing, mouths limp with drink,
hands clasped around each other – his
mates.
Shots of the seaman himself, challenging
life,
against a snow-covered mountain, in a grass
skirt,
with a beard, clean-shaven, in a Sombrero,
in jeans,
and then, in an ink-stained folder, with Mum
and Dad:
a middle-aged couple at home on a lawn,
Mum at the back door, Dad with his beans,
then the three together, on the beach at
Torquay,
when the sailor was sweet...and six years
old.

(2)

In innocence
playing football, watched by a fan
who stands, pipe in his mouth, a scarf
wrapped around his neck under his check
overcoat down to his knees. Sensible
shoes defy the hard mud from the field
and a slouch hat holds down his hair
in the wind cutting across the pitch.
His restless enthusiast's eyes glance
at the players jogging across the knuckled
grass and crust of mud. He sucks
in weary disgust as a kid makes
a stupid pass. Juniors versus juniors
in an afternoon game on the youth club's
ground.
The ball shoots across to the other side's
goal.
That goalkeeper's hair's too long. What's
this?
A debutante's dance? He saved it, though.
Not so bad, I suppose. Let's walk down his
end
for a different view...and a closer look.
Hmmm! A young kid. Body barely formed.
Clean.
Wonder why he's hair's so long. Those blond
streaks flaring our from his red-corduroy
cap
look untidy. Untidy? Well, a bit strange perhaps.

What a graceful neck. Goes well
with that bright green shirt. Good shoulders
too,
muscles rippling across sturdy back. Black
shorts
tightly covering comfortable buttocks. Ex-
panse
of brown leg, perfectly shaped, to thick light
blue socks
and cockeyed boots. A feline face
lost and alive to the game's excitement,
flushed
with activity. Beautiful! Out-of-breath chest
revealed
as the wind nips his shirt and cuffs him.
The game's nearly over but technique's ignored
by the football fan watching behind the goal.
A grey taste in his mouth, hands lost in his
coat,
he stares in a trance through the net at the
boy.
He sees youth for the first time in majesty
and his façade, wife and family pass him by.
He looks at the lad, at his sudden leaps,
at his vibrant frame, strapping legs, strip-
ling, stripping...
and wonders, in surprise, what he's like in
bed.

(3)

The seaman once saw a boy and wanted:
"I want to catch your gonorrhoea;
to join the embarrassed queue at the clinic
with a festering testimony of our frolic
when lust overcame discretion:
to have my own watering-can
like those ABs who qualify for men:
to enter the clinic and talk
to the ginger-haired doctor with the limp
sitting at his desk, in his white coat,
pen racing across a card with my number,
M 620,
as he listens to my systems:
discharge, blockage,
fluff getting stuck,
just like gravel when I piss;
to feel the nurse thumbing a vein
then plunging her needle to suck my blood
to fill a syringe for the doctor's test tube
and laboratory analysis;
to urinate behind a screen into a tiny jar
whistling for help at first
then wondering how to stop
as the excruciating pain reminds me of you
and I watch the tell-tale shreds.
Then go each Wednesday for a jab in my arse
and to take three pills a day at first
and then black and yellow bombs
as the disease sets in.
I want to be in torment through a delightful
night
when your body and peril were mine:
to catch your gonorrhoea and pretend I'm
a man."

(4)

I long to have sex between black leather
sheets
and ride shivering motorcycles through your
thighs.

I long to have sex on the sand in the sun
and smear myself as sun tan oil on your
body.

I long to have sex on an atlas
and wallow with you all over the world.

(5)

It was my idea
that I should go with him on this boat trip.
He said he was going to sail his sloop
down the coast of France from Le Havre to
Jersey
alone.
I hardly knew him
but he seemed a great sort of fellow
bubbling with life
and a bit of excitement like that
appealed to me.

We weren't at sea long
when the storm blew up.
We saw the dark clouds and rising waves
but there wasn't time to worry
and he seemed so beautifully confident.

It was over quickly;
this huge wave
towered above us then flopped down
and that was that.
I said we've had it,
clutched his waist
and then found myself in the water.
This bit of wood,
a plank from the deck we stood on together,
saved me for a second;
I looked around,
but he'd gone.

Memories flashed through my mind
and I wanted to struggle
then suddenly...
I split right open and cried with love
and knew how easy it all was.
A wave slapped me unconscious
and I ceased to exist.

THE CHERRY BOY
1967

A sequence of poems published by Turret Books,
London 1967, in an edition of 200 copies

For Julio.

You ask me what is poetry
fluttering your dark lashes
against mine.

You ask me what is poetry
when you are poetry yourself.

I was sailing through life
But I was lost
Until I saw the light of your eyes
Then the sky opened
and I had the whole world in my arms
But that's nothing for me
Because all that I have
Is only for you.

The two poems above were translated by
Royston Ellis from Spanish, the authors are not
known. The remaining poems were written in
Las Palmas, Canary Islands, in 1964, 1965 and
1966, and in Tortola, British Virgin Islands, 1967.
An extract from the poem "All my sex life"
appeared in *The Flesh Merchants* (Tandem Books,
1966) and version of "We are sitting" appeared
in *The Rush At The End* (Tandem Books, 1967).

THE CHERRY BOY

1.

All my sex life, I had been drifting
In and out of bed with beauties
Or old men who made it
Furtively worth my while,
For kicks, through boredom, but coolly
maintained, until lying in the sun of a
tropical isle
As one of the beach boys hustling
The tourists, masks melted, lusting
For every tan body, cartwheeling, lucky
Strike, blatantly whispering *fucky-fucky;*
I saw this beginner, his small body
Not even tanned, bristling, facing
The hard horizon of sex beyond the beach –
Thighs of the asthmatic Canadian,
Wallet of the queen from Morecombe,
Lips of the crewcut American plater,
Hands of the impotent Brighton bookmaker –
Nervously following the others.

Suddenly,
Crushingly older, I carried him off the beach
In a vain attempt to save youth from the
streets
For his innocence was worth more than
those men would pay.

Now the season has ended, the tourists
gone,
And the beach boys are having each other

For free... In those months I watched him
evolve
From a cherry boy to a man, cool, a sexual
Cashbox registering with a mechanical kiss
Through pursed lips, the cost of short times.
For five more years, he'll be available as
My battered body once was.
Now I: shattered, the old man forced to pay,
He: the young body paid to oblige.

Retired, every night at his initiation, I feel
Him still in my arms, on my lips, in my life;
And find it hard to believe that my youth
was real.

2.

We're never so beautiful before
    As we are afterwards...

When our enthusiasm has mellowed us,
When your hair is ruffled in curls
And your eyes, tired and happy, smile at the
dark.
When your body, too lazy to move,
Stays close to me, and I feel
The warmth of that moment beating out
of you.

You lie there, clasping my hand
unconsciously in yours,
Lips apart,
Blankets thrown back; the sheet
Covering your sun-limbed body.

I drink you in and smile with you.

It all breaks, of course, when you go to
the bathroom
To wash me away, comb your hair,
Come back and finish your unfinished drink
Pick up your cigarette and re-light it.

You look at me and say you're going.

I reach out of bed for my trousers,
Take out pesetas and give them to you.

See you tomorrow, you say, counting,
And you go.

3.

And then one night we discovered kissing.

We peered behind the curtains of our cabin
window
At the farewell crowds gathered on the quay,
Fearing your father would arrive with
an escort
To prohibit our private voyage.

We were holding hands
Huddled together on the upper bunk
Forgetting your formalities of love;
Standards of your way of life.

The gangway was up,
Bells, splashing ropes, and shouts from
the quay
As slowly the ship began to pull away:
The hot intimacy of our joint concern
Blazing suddenly into fire.

That was the night we discovered kissing.

4.

What I like
Is the way you run
Your clenched hands across your eyes
Grinding your knuckles into the soft flesh
As though to squeeze me out
But I am still curled around you
And in you
And I hurt.
That's what I like.

5.

We are sitting in a room
    With the world around us.

We are waiting in a womb
    With new sounds about us.

We are wrapped around with entrails
    Of the women who bore us,
    Our bodies wet with the flow of fathers
    When in innocent days they loved
    for us.

We are coiled in a spring
    With life busy about us.

Soon the time will be
    When we will be
    And then those busy sounds
    Will die and we
    Unwinding from the wounds
    Will leap into reality.

We are sitting in a room
    Chemistry working in us
    To become, to become, to become.

An alligator crawls around my head,
    Porpoises leap in your eyes,
    Tortoises chip at my teeth
    And peacocks strut on your knees.
Now we know we are free!

6.

It was an international rage
Sweeping the youth of Europe, the world
Of young men involved with music,
Clothes, sex: a pursuit of enjoyment
As the only aim in a boredom of affluence.

It was a convenient kick
More mature than drinking, keener than
pills,
And a brotherhood from Istanbul to
San Juan
Which turned us on to that softer life.
We smoked together confidently
Appreciating the affection billowing
around us.

And then, blow by blow, as the season months
Stole by, you grew out of me
With visions and mind-blocked dreams
Of a trip you must take to understand
The influences of your pituitary gland.

A Norwegian girl's hands groping on a car
backseat,
A French virgin succumbing at night on the
beach,
an American widow, a typist who's Swiss,
An English air hostess, a German gym
mistress,
A growling Dutch lesbian with contact
lenses,
And a dozen Swedish chicks in studied
frenzies.

The cherry boy, once the sweetest prize,
Was growing bitter before my eyes.

7.

On the tarmac, jets and smaller planes
Pause in the sun while the sea
Just beyond the runway, glistens.
In the restaurant beyond the terrace,
the tannoy
Erupts in three indistinct languages about
the boy.

He leans across the table, placing his
slender hand
On my arm. We grin
As a chartered flight straightens out on
the runway
With another group of cut-price tourists
from Sweden.
He goes soon. We have no words now.
The girls with us watch, sipping the
champagne
They have bought us. He blinks in thought.

He is different now. Different from the
boy who lay
On the beach just a week before.
Nervous, pale, a ghost from that day
When he was proffered help by an eager
woman
To escape in return for various favours.

He has told me of his life to be
On the streets of Stockholm
        Acting out ambitions
        In centrally-heated apartments
In Copenhagen, Helsinki, Hamburg
and Oslo.

For money
    It is all right
To be cool; never to love. Gaining
A fortune at poking to spend it on smoking.

He has decided and he has said
To those who dreamed on the sands
That it is better to lie in bed
Than lie dreaming of other lands.

A propeller revs up cautiously, shimmers
Floating in front of the morning sun.
He leans across the table, placing his
slender hand
On my arm, fingers feeling for mine.
I turn away so he can catch his plane
And the girls sip their champagne with
a sigh
As the tannoy echoes the last goodbye.

Passengers to Stockholm are requested to
proceed...

THE END

BOOKS BY ROYSTON ELLIS

Poetry:
Jiving To Gyp
Rave
The Rainbow Walking Stick
The Mattress Flowers
Burn Up (concert performance script)
The Cherry Boy

Biography:
Driftin' With Cliff Richard
Rebel, the Story of James Dean
The Big Beat Scene
The Shadows By Themselves
A Man for All Islands (President Gayoom of Maldives)
My Log Book (Ali Maniku)
Toni, the Maldives Lady
The Growing Years (History of the Ceylon Planters' Assoc.)
Twenty Years Uncovered, The MAS Story

Travel:
India By Rail
Sri Lanka By Rail
Seeing Sri Lanka By Train
Bradt Guides to Mauritius
Bradt Guides to Maldives
Bradt Guides to Sri Lanka
On The Wings of Freedom
The Story of the Grand Hotel
The Story of the Tea Factory Hotel
The Story of the Bandarawela Hotel
The Sri Lanka Story
The Story of Full Moon, Maldives
A Maldives Celebration

Insight Pocket Guides to Maldives
Insight Guides to Sri Lanka
Sri Lanka Step By Step
Festivals of the World: Trinidad
Festivals of the World: Madagascar
Berlitz Pocket Guide to Maldives
The Kurumba Story
Baros The Legend

Fiction: Myself For Fame
The Flesh Merchants
The Flesh Game (USA)
The Rush At The End
A Hero In Time

(as *Richard Tresillian*)
The Bondmaster
Blood of the Bondmaster
The Bondmaster Breed
Bondmaster Buck
Bondmaster Revenge
Bondmaster Fury
Fleur
Giselle
Bloodheart
Bloodheart Royal
Bloodheart Feud

(as *Raynard Devine*)
Master of Black River
Black River Affair
Black River Breed

RAVE (GONE MAN SQUARED) The world's first beat perfume, a deliciously unusual concoction with hints of coffee and cardamom. Packaged with vintage typewriter key charm.

Alluring scent for women and men. Generous 1/2 ounce perfume in exquisite glass vial with presentation box.

Send All Orders to KICKS BOOKS CO., P.O. Box 646 Cooper Station, NY NY 10276

KICKS BOOKS PRESENTS...

Kicks Magazine Rock & Roll Photo Album #1
The Great Lost Photographs of Eddie Rocco

Fabulous collection of previously unpublished photographs by Charlton Publications photographer Eddie Rocco! Sepia-toned trade paperback includes photo tribute to Kicks icon Esquerita plus other favorites including Redd Foxx, Ruth Brown, the Treniers, Jackie Wilson, Johnny Otis, the Beach Boys, Jan & Dean, the Byrds and more!

NECESSARY

WHILE THEY LAST

**Alluring scents for women and men.
Generous 1/2 ounce perfume in exquisite
glass vial with presentation box.**

RAVE (GONE MAN SQUARED) The world's first beat perfume, a deliciously unusual concoction with hints of coffee and cardamom. Packaged with vintage typewriter key charm.

SIN TIME (GETTING IN THE WIND) Venial vixens will find that this exotic elixer evokes excitement at any hour of the day or nite. This big girl scent is equally magnetic for big boys. A pair of tiny dice inside the bottle add a dash to the splash.

GARBAGE (LORD OF GARBAGE) The brooding complexity of Kim Fowley's signature scent is reflected in this fruity but absurd potion that suits lads and

Send All Orders to KICKS BOOKS CO.,

SPACE IS THE PLACE!
Sun Ra on Norton

Harlan Ellison is
OUT FOR KICKS!

All hail the master of original street action JD fiction –
dig Harlan Ellison's rarest genre-scorching killers delivered
in a menacing pair of hip-pocket paperbacks!

OTHER KICKS BOOKS
YOU WILL ENJOY

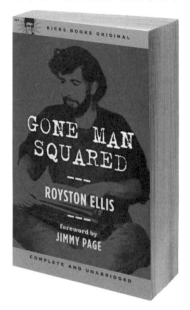

KB1 *Sweets and Other Stories* by Andre Williams
KB2 *This Planet is Doomed* by Sun Ra
KB3 *Save The Last Dance For Satan* by Nick Tosches
KB4 *Pulling A Train* by Harlan Ellison
KB5 *Lord of Garbage* by Kim Fowley
KB6 *Getting in the Wind* by Harlan Ellison
KB7 *Gone Man Squared* by Royston Ellis

WILLIAMS · SUN RA · TOSCHES
ELLISON · FOWLEY · ELLIS

KICKS BOOKS
PO BOX 646 COOPER STATION,
NEW YORK NY 10276
www.kicksbooks.com